OZZIE SMITH
The Road to Cooperstown

OZZIE SMITH *with Rob Rains*
Foreword by Whitey Herzog

OZZIE SMITH

The Road to Cooperstown

Hall of Fame Limited Edition

Sports Publishing L.L.C.
Publisher: **Peter L. Bannon**
Senior Managing Editors: **Joseph J. Bannon, Jr. and Susan M. Moyer**
Art Director: **K. Jeffrey Higgerson**

Graphic Designer: **Christine Mohrbacher**
Acquisition Editor: **Bob Snodgrass**
Developmental Editor: **Scott Rauguth**
Copy Editor: **Cynthia L. McNew**

Printed in Canada

Front cover photos: Counter clockwise from the top,
Mary Butkus, AP/Wide World Photos;
Mark J. Terrill, AP/Wide World Photos;
AP/Wide World Photos;
Provided by Ozzie Smith
Back cover photo: **Beth A. Keiser, AP/Wide World Photos**

ISBN: 1-58261-598-5

This book is dedicated to my three children, O.J., Dustin and Taryn. Thanks for your love and understanding.
- Ozzie Smith

Ozzie Smith, this year's only inductee into the Baseball Hall of Fame, answers a question on Tuesday, May 28, 2002, at the Hall of Fame in Cooperstown. (AP Photo/Jim McKnight)

Foreword

By Whitey Herzog

Former St. Louis Cardinals shortstop Ozzie Smith and manager Whitey Herzog. (Bill Greenblatt, UPI)

When most people think about Ozzie Smith, they think about a time they were either at the ballpark or watching a game on television and saw him make a great play. I saw him play shortstop almost every day for nine years, and when I think about those games, there is something else that stands out.

I don't think about the great plays, and we all know there were a lot of them. I think about all of the routine plays, how he made them night after night, game after game, and how he never messed them up. I can only remember one time when he got an error on a play he should have made—one time in thousands of chances. That's how good a player he was—a Hall of Famer. I don't see how you can play the position any better than he played it. He didn't have the greatest arm in the world, but even when he hurt his arm, he made adjustments and was still able to make all of the plays.

I was fortunate to see Marty Marion and Luis Aparicio play and they were great shortstops. Were they better than Ozzie? I don't think so. The one common bond they all shared, however, was how steady they were, how they were able to get the job done every game.

What set Ozzie apart was his ability to make the great play and his ability to energize the fans. People really did come to the ballpark to watch him play. We would be on the road, in Atlanta or Pittsburgh or someplace, and people would be there wearing an Ozzie Smith jersey. He was good at what he did, but he also had a flare and a style about him that made the fans love him.

When we were able to bring Ozzie over from San Diego, it was the final piece of the puzzle in making the Cardinals a championship club. I did tell Ozzie that if he would agree to the trade, I thought we would have a team that could win the World Series. We were lucky enough to do that in 1982, and we won two more pennants in the next five years as well.

When we made the trade, I didn't know that Ozzie would become a Hall of Famer. He was able to do that, I believe, because he worked hard at making himself a better player. As good as he was defensively, he was still out there every night before a game, taking extra ground balls, working on covering second base, performing all of the routine tasks a lot of major leaguers forget to work on.

Ozzie's hard work really set a tone for the other players on our team as well. When youngsters like Willie McGee and Vince Coleman and Terry Pendleton came up and saw how hard Ozzie was working, they correctly figured that was how hard they needed to work as well. All of that work made us a better team.

The other intangible benefit Ozzie brought to the Cardinals was his off-the-field work with all of those young guys. Coming to the major leagues for the first time can be a very scary and lonely feeling. Ozzie kept those guys with him, made sure they ate at good restaurants and got their rest, and looked after them the way an older brother would.

Another reason Ozzie became a Hall of Famer was his hard work on offense. I was frequently quoted early in his career in St. Louis, saying how important I thought he was to our club because of his tremendous defense. If he saved two runs a game on defense, which he did many a night, it seemed to me that was just as valuable to the team as a player who drove in two runs a game on offense. Ozzie wasn't satisfied with that,

though. He also wanted to be a good offensive player. He worked and got stronger, and as he understood the game better, he was able to make big contributions with the bat.

I was proud to be his manager, and I am proud of him now. I managed one Hall of Famer in Kansas City, George Brett, and now Ozzie has earned his place beside George in Cooperstown. It's an honor he richly deserves.

Whitey Herzog

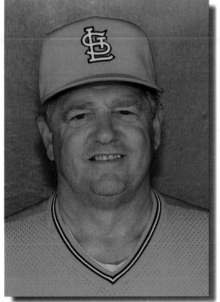

(AP Photo)

I wish I had a nickel for every time I have been introduced as "future Hall of Famer Ozzie Smith" over the past five years. It would add up to a lot of nickels.

It seems that ever since I retired, and actually for several years before that, people made the assumption that I would be elected to the Hall of Fame. I never let myself get carried away with all that talk, mainly because it was a decision which was out of my control.

I didn't begin my baseball career to become a Hall of Famer. I didn't bounce the ball off the concrete steps of my home in south central Los Angeles as a young boy thinking one day I would be walking into the shrine in Cooperstown, New York.

In high school, in college, or in Walla Walla, Washington, I didn't think about the Hall of Fame. I didn't think about it when I broke into the major leagues with the San Diego Padres, or even after I was traded to the St. Louis Cardinals.

Even after I had been in the major leagues for several years and achieved some success, my driving force was never to become a Hall of Famer. My goal was to be the best player I could be, and if that was good enough for me to be a Hall of Famer, then that was what I wanted to be.

Fame

NATIONAL BASEBALL HALL OF FAME AND MUSEUM

December 19, 2001

Mr. Ozzie Smith

Dear Ozzie:

On behalf of The National Baseball Hall of Fame and Museum's **Board of Directors**, congratulations on being selected by the Baseball Writers Association of America's Screening Committee for consideration on the 2002 Hall of Fame ballot.

Only 15,500 individuals over the 125 years of baseball history have had the privilege of playing in the Major Leagues, and less than one percent have been elected to The National Baseball Hall of Fame.

Should you earn election to the Hall of Fame, we want you to know it is our policy that the Museum will decide which logo appears on your plaque. Major League Baseball endorses this policy, played will be listed within its text.

The National Baseball Hall of Fame and Museum is a not-for-profit, educational institution dedicated to fostering an appreciation of the historical development of baseball and its impact on our culture by collecting, preserving, exhibiting and interpreting its collections for a global audience as well as honoring those who have made outstanding contributions to our National Pastime.

My best wishes to you.

Sincerely,

Dale

Dale Petroskey
President

25 MAIN STREET, P.O. BOX 590, COOPERSTOWN, NEW YORK 13326-0590
(607) 547-7200   FAX (607) 547-2044
baseballhalloffame.org

"I did not think I would be that overwelmed when I got that phone call."

The Hall of Fame rules require a player to wait five years after he retires before he is eligible to be elected. The voting panel is comprised of ten-year (minimum) members of the Baseball Writers Association of America. To be elected, a player must receive 75 percent of the ballots cast.

Former St. Louis shortstop Ozzie Smith smiles as he takes questions and reflects on his baseball career Wednesday, Jan. 9, 2002, during a news conference in New York. (AP Photo/Beth A. Keiser)

Ozzie looks on as St. Louis Cardinals partial owner Fred Hanser introduces him at a news conference announcing Smith's selection to the National Baseball Hall of Fame, Tuesday, Jan. 8, 2001, in Eureka, Mo. (AP Photo/Tom Gannam)

In the days leading up to the election announcement on January 8, 2002, I had people come up and tell me not to be disappointed if I was not elected on the first ballot. I really didn't know how to react to that, because I had other people telling me I was a shoo-in.

When you know that a telephone call is coming, the wait can be excruciating. I knew that if I had been elected, I would get a phone call with that information. If the phone didn't ring, all of the guests who had assembled in my house were going to go out for lunch.

The call came. Jack O'Connell, the secretary of the BBWAA, delivered the news that I had received 92 percent of the votes cast. I was a Hall of Famer.

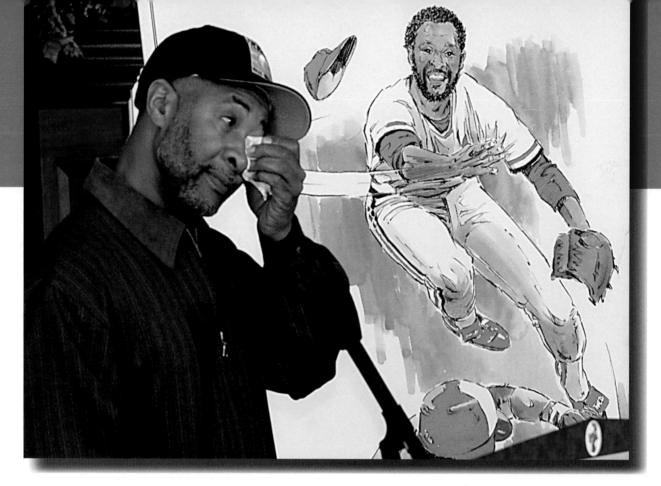

*Ozzie pauses to wipe his eyes during the news
conference announcing his selection to the National
Baseball Hall of Fame. (AP Photo/Tom Gannam)*

I had gone over it a thousand times in my mind—the way it would come about.
The only thing I miscalculated was the degree of emotion that would overwhelm me.
When I hung up the phone and saw all of the people in the room smiling and about
to go crazy, the tears began to flow.

Crying is strange. I don't know the reasons why people cry when they are happy,
but it happens. I did not think I would be that overwhelmed when I got that phone call.

We opened a bottle of champagne I had saved for a special occasion, and I spent
some time talking on the telephone. One of the first calls of congratulations came from
the baseball commissioner, Bud Selig.

Ozzie, left, gets a warm reception from former manager Whitey Herzog.
(AP Photo/Tom Gannam)

When I addressed the media later that afternoon for a news conference, I became emotional again. Even though the news had sunk in a little in the few hours that had passed since the phone call, when I started talking about it again, the tears flowed one more time.

Even though I thought I had a good chance of being elected, I never would have guessed that I would be the only player elected this year. There were some other very worthy candidates on the ballot, including Gary Carter, Jim Rice, Bruce Sutter and Andre Dawson. But for only the third time since 1965, the writers elected only one player. Willie Stargell and Reggie Jackson were the only other players to go into the Hall of Fame alone in the last 37 years, so I am in some pretty elite company.

Ozzie speaks in front of a large portrait of himself during the news conference.
(AP Photo/Tom Gannam)

Left: St. Louis Cardinals great
Ozzie Smith speaks during
the news conference.
(AP Photo/Tom Gannam)

Right: Ozzie jokes with
reporters when asked to do
a flip, which he did not, after
a news conference in New York.
Smith will be inducted into this
year's Baseball Hall of Fame for
his two decades as one of
the games best shortstops
for the San Diego Padres
and St. Louis Cardinals.
(AP Photo/Beth A. Keiser)

I think my vote total and election addressed the impact that I had at my position. By playing great defense, I brought attention to myself and to the position of shortstop. If my election to the Hall of Fame does anything, I hope it will allow more people to be recognized for what they achieve defensively, because I think that especially in this current era defense is a skill which is often overlooked.

Playing good defense came easy to me, but it was also something I worked hard at every day. Even after I had made it to the major leagues, won Gold Gloves, and been elected to the All-Star team, I made certain I went out and had plenty of fielding practice before every game. I caught ground balls going to my right, I caught ground

Ozzie Smith

balls going to my left, I worked on making the pivot at second base and I worked on my reactions to the ball by having coaches fire throws at me from short range while I was on my knees.

Some of that work rubbed off on others. I think a lot of young players especially noticed that here I was, an established and successful major leaguer, and here was how hard I was working. They knew they had to work too, and the result made us a better team.

One thing about the Hall of Fame is that it is a singular honor. Baseball is a team game. I didn't win games, pennants, or the World Series by myself. I won as part of a team, and I am grateful for all of the teammates I had during my career. Each and every one of them played a role in getting me where I am today.

Ozzie Smith, this year's only inductee into the Baseball Hall of Fame, poses on Tuesday, May 28, 2002, at the Hall of Fame in Cooperstown, N.Y. Behind his right shoulder is a glove he wore during his 19-year major league career. At the right is Smith doing one of his famous backflips. The "Wizard of Oz" will be inducted on Sunday, July 28 in Cooperstown.
(AP Photo/Jim McKnight)

Torchbearer Ozzie Smith carries the Olympic Flame. He and St. Louis Rams quarterback Kurt Warner light the Olympic cauldron during the Olympic Torch celebration Tuesday, Jan. 8, 2002, in St. Louis. (AP Photo/Todd Warshaw, Pool)

From left to right: AP Photo/Tom Gannam; AP Photo/Todd Warshaw; AP Photo/Tom Gannam

It was ironic that the day the Hall of Fame announcement was scheduled happened to be the same day the Olympic torch was coming through St. Louis on its way to Salt Lake City for the winter Games. The organizers asked me to help carry the torch through downtown and light the caldron in Kiener Plaza that would remain lit overnight before the torch run began again the next morning.

Talk about a special day! Getting the call to tell me I had been elected to the Hall of Fame in the morning, then carrying the Olympic torch at night. It was a special night for me and for St. Louis. I went to bed that night a happy man.

Growing up in south central Los Angeles and making it to the Hall of Fame: that is the stuff dreams are made of. Anything that you dream of, if you put your mind to it and dedicate yourself to it and work for it, you can achieve it. I know. It happened to me.

"I have been privileged to carry the Olympic Torch three times. It really is a special moment, but you spend most of the time trying to make sure you don't drop it."
–Ozzie

Wizard of Oz

People often wonder what their lives would have been like had they made a different decision at some point in time. I have made several of those life-altering choices, starting with the decision not to sign with the Detroit Tigers when I was drafted after my junior year in college.

"We had a pretty good team in college at Cal Poly.
I am in the middle of the front row." –Ozzie

Div. II District 8 Regional Playoffs
Southern Calif. Alliance Championship

1977

41–20

OZZIE SMITH

"Learning the proper technique for catching a ground ball was a key to my early success." –Ozzie

"When I first began to do the backflips in San Diego, I had no idea it would become my trademark." –Ozzie

Instead, I went back to school and signed a year later with the San Diego Padres. One year later, I was in the major leagues. That choice obviously worked out well.

Four years later, another decision had to be made—whether to waive a no-trade provision in my contract and accept a trade to the Cardinals, or block the deal and remain in San Diego. I really went back and forth trying to decide.

What finally convinced me to OK the trade was a personal visit from Whitey Herzog, who flew out to San Diego and talked me into becoming a Cardinal. Whitey told me that if I came to St. Louis, the Cardinals would win a World Series. I could tell immediately that Whitey was the type of manager for whom I wanted to play, and the trade sending me to the Cardinals and Garry Templeton to the Padres was completed.

Ozzie signs one of his first major league autographs at Padres Spring Training in Yuma, AZ., 1978. (David Simpson)

"Still, one of my goals when I made it to the major leagues was to become the best offensive player I could be."

The Wizard (ry) of Oz

Ozzie Smith, already showing his defensive prowess with the Padres, in this feature done by the Yuma Daily Sun in March, 1981. (David Simpson)

No one will ever know what would have happened had I decided to remain in San Diego. I don't know if I would have won a World Series, and I don't know if I would have been elected to the Hall of Fame. Luckily, we don't ever have to find out.

I enjoyed my time with the Padres, and I had a lot of great things happen to me while I was there. I set the assist record for shortstops in a single season, and I know I would have had a chance to play and perform well. I could have won Gold Gloves and made the All-Star team, but I don't know if I would have improved as much offensively as I did with the Cardinals.

I never will forget one occasion, early in my career with the Padres, when I went to our hitting coach for some advice. I asked him what I should do with my hands if I was trying to hit the ball up the middle. Should I pull them down, or try to turn them over, or what exactly should my approach be? He just looked back at me and said, "Forget all that stuff; just aim up the middle."

Because I was always small physically, I was not gifted as a hitter. I was never the biggest or strongest guy on my team, and luckily I was a good enough defensive player that most of my coaches never worried about my offense. Still, one of my goals when I made it to the major leagues was to become the best offensive player I could be.

I know Lou Brock used to get upset, and probably still does, when people labeled him a one-dimensional player, thinking all he could do was run fast and steal bases. Well, he had to get on base before he could steal second or third, and he did that by collecting more than 3,000 hits in his career. He was definitely not a one-dimensional player.

The tag immediately placed on me was that I was a "defensive" player. Early in my career, that was probably an accurate label. Playing defense had always come easily to me, starting from the time I was a young boy growing up in south central Los Angeles.

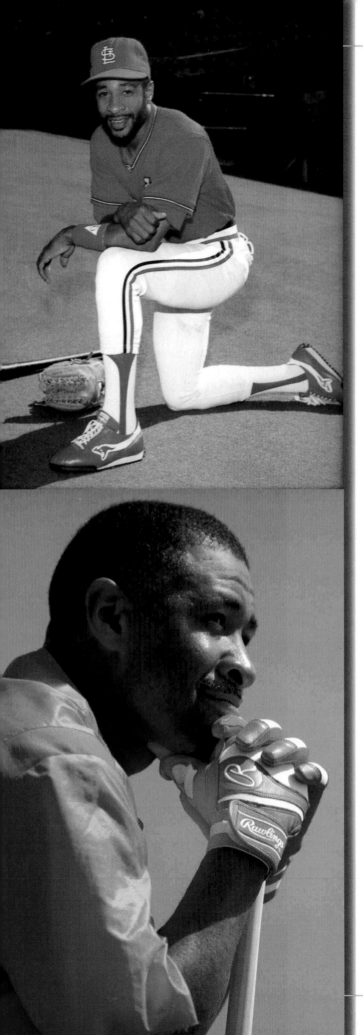

Whenever I wasn't playing with the other kids in the neighborhood, I would play games by myself. I honestly believe that in addition to being blessed by God with great hand-eye coordination and quickness, some of those games I played when I was a young boy played a major role in the development of my skills.

I always had a ball and a glove in my hand. If I wasn't playing catch by bouncing the ball off the concrete steps in front of our house, always moving in closer so I would have less time to react and catch the ball, I was bouncing it off the wall of our garage. When I got tired of that, I would lie down and throw the ball up in the air, then close my eyes and try to catch it. I broke a few windows, and I got yelled at, but I cleaned up the mess and kept on playing.

Ozzie takes a break before batting practice Saturday, Feb. 24, 1996, at Busch Complex in St. Petersburg, Fla. (AP Photo/Susan Sterner)

Another game I played by myself was to stand in the front yard, throw the ball over the roof, and try to race around to the back yard and catch it before it hit the ground. I never caught it, but I got close plenty of times.

Believing that I actually could catch the ball was important to me. I always believed that I could be successful, but along with that belief was a knowledge that it wouldn't happen without a lot of hard work. I realize that I was very blessed by everything that happened to me during my career, but I also know how hard I worked to make myself better.

I developed a kind of philosophy at some point in my career that "nothing is good enough if it can be made better." The extension of that was that better was not good enough if it could be the best. I had one goal—to be the best I could be—and that applied to everything I did.

My nickname is the Wizard, which naturally came from the movie *The Wizard of Oz*. There was actually a point in my life and career when I really didn't care much for that name, but the longer I played, and the more things I experienced in baseball and in life, the more I realized that the nickname really was an extension of my life.

Think about the characters in the movie. What did the scarecrow want? A brain. The tin man wanted a heart. The lion was searching for courage. Really, those three characteristics were the keys to my success—I had a mind to dream that I could be a major leaguer, the heart to believe in myself, and the courage to pursue that dream.

There are certain skills which a person needs to be a successful baseball player. The players whom I consider the most successful in the game, however, are those that go beyond raw physical talent. They have other innate talents which carry them to the next level.

San Francisco Giant Barry Bonds, left, and former
St. Louis Cardinals shortstop Ozzie Smith talk at
Busch Stadium in St. Louis, Friday, June 22, 2001.
(AP Photo/James A. Finley)

Ozzie looks on from the dugout during batting
practice before Game 7 of the National League
Championship Series in Atlanta Thursday,
Oct. 17, 1996. (AP Photo/Dave Martin)

Those kinds of players have character. They have pride. They possess dignity. They respect the game and earn respect in return. They are selfless. They realize that important accomplishments are nice, but that the ultimate in this game is winning as a team. They make the commitment to work hard to reach that goal.

That is the kind of player I wanted to be, especially after Whitey motivated me into accepting the trade to the Cardinals and instilled that drive in me to become the best player I could be.

"The stained glass front door of my house reminds me every day of my life's journey. Each star is inscribed with a special moment in ...

"The way I played was the way our entire team played."

"I really never thought I would finish my career with more than 2,000 hits."
—Ozzie

I know Whitey was worried that I would change my mind and try to cancel the deal when I came to St. Louis to sign the contract and hold my first news conference as a Cardinal in February of 1982. I don't think I had ever been that cold, and I know I had never seen as much snow in my life. The photographers even took us outside to take pictures of us throwing snowballs. The baseball season doesn't start until April, however, and I thought the snow would probably melt by then.

The more I was around Whitey, the better I liked him, and I am proud we still have a great relationship today. What he did for me, more than anything, was motivate me. He didn't want me to accept being a .250 hitter if I could be a .260 or .270 hitter, and not to accept that if I could do better.

That first spring training, he came up with a challenge for me that we carried over into the regular season. Every time I hit the ball on the ground, he would pay me a dollar. Every time

I popped up or hit the ball in the air, I would owe him a dollar.

He was trying to make me concentrate on hitting the ball on the ground, which was the way he thought I could be the most successful offensively. One of Whitey's greatest traits was that he always tried to put his players in a position where they had the greatest chance of being successful, and this was just another example of that.

I don't think either Whitey or I ever thought the ploy would work out so well. It really forced me to concentrate on my approach to hitting, and there were many nights when Whitey had to pay me $4. He paid up every night, too. I think I was about $300 ahead for the year when he finally called off the deal.

Little things like that were what made Whitey so successful, and he made baseball fun. Baseball can be a lousy game when you are doing poorly and the team is losing, but you can't imagine how much fun it is when you are doing well and the team is winning.

That was exactly what happened that season. The way I played was the way our entire team played. We didn't have a lot of guys who could hit home runs, especially the way Busch Stadium played then, and Whitey convinced everybody that we would be successful if we kept the ball on the ground, used our speed to get on base, stole bases every chance we got, and played good defense. The media even came up with a word for it—Whiteyball. We had many times when someone would get on base with a walk, steal second, have a ground ball to second move him to third, and he would score on a sacrifice fly. We had a run without a single hit.

Whitey assigned our third-base coach, Chuck Hiller, to work with me, and I also spent a lot of time with Dave Ricketts. Dave officially had the title of bullpen coach, but he was more than that. He was always available when guys needed extra batting practice, and he was the guy who really taught me how to keep my hands on top of the ball. That way I wasn't always swinging under the ball, hitting popups, but was hitting either line drives or ground balls. I really understood the concept of what he was teaching me.

Ozzie stands next to his jersey in the team clubhouse in St. Louis. The Cardinals announced that his uniform, No.1, would be retired. (AP Photo/James A. Finley)

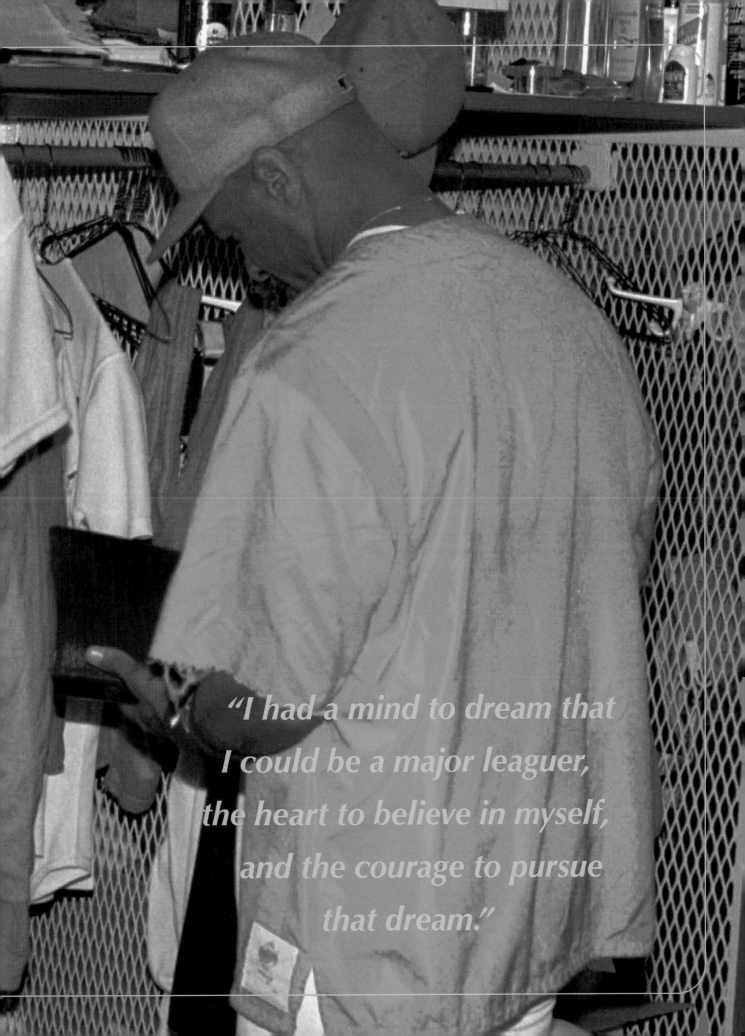

"I had a mind to dream that
I could be a major leaguer,
the heart to believe in myself,
and the courage to pursue
that dream."

Cleveland Indians base runner Kenny Lofton and Ozzie look to umpire Charlie Reliford for the call on a pickoff play at second base in the sixth inning of the All-Star Game Tuesday, July 9, 1996, in Philadelphia's Veterans Stadium. (AP Photo/Roberto Borea)

Dave had all kinds of drills to remind me where my hands needed to be, and all of that repetition really carried over into the games. For the first time I understood what I was trying to do at the plate.

The only guy on our team who hit more than 12 homers was George Hendrick, my former teammate in San Diego, who hit 19. We stole 200 bases, the most in the National League, and our starting infield of Keith Hernandez at first, Tom Herr at second, Ken Oberkfell at third and me at shortstop combined to make only 44 errors for the entire season.

I don't know why, but I think defense has generally been overlooked as a necessary component of a winning team. In addition to making me concentrate more on hitting the ball on the ground that year, one of the other things Whitey did for me and for baseball in general was to recognize how important playing great defense was to our success.

Whitey was quoted often that year as saying some of my defensive plays had saved us one or more runs a game, and that preventing those runs from scoring was in reality just as important as driving in runs. They don't have a statistic for that—runs saved by great defense—but Whitey made certain everybody in baseball knew that was one of the reasons we were winning.

"People talk about all of the great plays I made in my career, but I really am proud of all of the routine ones as well." –Ozzie

Another great thing that happened that year was the birth of a relationship which has endured for more than 20 years—my friendship with Willie McGee.

At the start of the 1982 season, we thought our center fielder was going to be David Green, a young phenom who looked like he had all the talent in the world. Willie had come over from the Yankees as a minor leaguer during the off season, and after spring training he was sent to Triple A so that he would have a chance to play every day.

David got hurt in May, and Willie was brought up to fill his place on the roster. When Whitey met with him, he told Willie he didn't really think he would be in the majors very long, probably only until David was healthy enough to play again. The Cardinals liked Willie well enough; they just thought David was a little more advanced at that point in their careers.

My wife Denise and I had gotten to know Willie a little during spring training, and because we knew he would be alone and kind of in awe of the major leagues, we asked if he wanted to stay with us instead of staying in a hotel. That two-week stay turned into two years.

Willie and I became close for a lot of reasons. Being together gave us a chance to talk about baseball, and I think I was able to take his mind off the game at times as well so that he wasn't getting so wound up and worried all the time. Willie is a sensitive guy, and I recognized that pretty quickly. Whitey jokes that Willie is the kind of player who can get three hits in a game and then cry because he didn't get a fourth hit.

Since I was new to the team as well, Willie also became important to my success. I had a friend I could relax with, and we just had a good time, whether we were hanging out at home, on the road or at the ballpark.

One difference for me in coming to St. Louis was that I had never been on a good team before. My rookie year in San Diego, we finished a few games above .500 but were still in fourth place. Then we were just bad—losing 90-plus games one year and finishing last twice.

What I learned in St. Louis was that just as losing can become a habit, so can winning. We won 12 games in a row in April, and it was an unbelievable experience—until I remembered we still had five more months to play. What happened during that winning streak, however, was that our team developed a positive attitude—that we knew we were good and could win. Again, it got back to the idea of believing in ourselves and our manager believing in us and doing what he could to make us successful.

By the middle of the year it was obvious to me that we were going to be in the pennant race all year, and I was excited. As we reached September, we were still battling for first, and finally, with a week to play, we clinched the division title in Montreal. All we had to do was beat the Braves in the playoffs and we would be playing in the World Series.

The fans in St. Louis were going crazy. I knew from my days as a visiting player coming into St. Louis that it was a good baseball town, but those Cardinal teams were a little down, so I think some of the enthusiasm was missing from the fans. As soon as we started to win, however, here came the fans—and they are still coming. Many people consider St. Louis to be the best baseball city in the country, and that's how I cast my vote too. One of the biggest reasons is the support of the fans. They really do

Ozzie acknowledges the crowd after tying the all-time mark for double plays by shortstops held by Luis Aparicio in the fourth inning, in St. Louis, Monday, Sept. 11, 1995. Smith already owns baseball's all-time record for assists by a shortstop, and he is the National League record holder for games played and double plays. (AP Photo/Mary Butkus)

"Many people consider St. Louis to be the best baseball city in the country, and that's how I cast my vote too."

Ozzie Smith looks back to the crowd after receiving a standing ovation in the seventh inning of the All-Star Game Tuesday, July 9, 1996, in Philadelphia's Veterans Stadium. This was the last All-Star Game for Smith who announced his retirement earlier this season.
(AP Photo/Susan Walsh)

support you when you are doing well, but they are also there encouraging you and cheering when you are doing poorly. All they want is a good effort and to believe that you are trying your best. That is why players such as Rex Hudler and Jose Oquendo were so popular in St. Louis. They weren't the most skilled players physically, but the fans loved them because they played the game so hard and had so much desire. It was really fun to see.

We did beat the Braves, three games in a row, so we moved on to the 1982 World Series to face Milwaukee. Because this was all a new experience for me, I had no idea what to expect. I didn't really think I was nervous, but I knew they would be the most important baseball games I had ever played, and I really wanted to do my best. You had to approach it like it was just another game, but it really was impossible to do that, especially when the series went to a seventh and deciding game.

"Baseball was a better game because of the contributions of people like Harry Caray." –Ozzie

Willie and I drove to the ballpark together, and I told him that the next night we would be celebrating as world champions. He told me that if somebody had told him a year earlier where he would be at that moment, he would have thought he was dreaming. We celebrated after a 6-3 win gave us the title and fulfilled the promise Whitey had made to me nine months earlier.

We had a ticker-tape parade through downtown St. Louis the next day, and I have never seen so many happy people in one place in my life. The grin on my face should have told everybody that I was one of the happiest people there.

One of the reasons I was so happy was because I thought Whitey had put together a team that was going to be more than just a one-year wonder. There was no reason we couldn't go out and win again the following season and for years to come. As is often the case in baseball, however, I found out that repeating as champion is not easy.

In fact, it was three more years before we won again, in 1985. I think the 1985 squad was probably the best team I was on during my career. We had some key guys remaining from the 1982 club, but we also made a few changes. We had traded Keith Hernandez to the Mets, and we later acquired Jack Clark to play first base. Tommy and I were still together, and we had replaced Oberkfell, traded to Atlanta, with a young player named Terry Pendleton.

Willie was still in center, and in left we had a rookie, Vince Coleman, who kind of appeared on the scene the same way Willie had in 1982. He also came up because of an injury, this time to Willie, and was only expected to stay around a couple of weeks. He played so well and provided such a spark at the top of the lineup that he stayed, and Whitey made a place for him by trading Lonnie Smith to Kansas City. George Hendrick had been traded to Pittsburgh for John Tudor, so Andy Van Slyke and Tito Landrum were platooning out there. Darrell Porter was still our catcher.

"I was fortunate to have some great friends as my teammates, including Willie McGee and Vince Coleman. I wonder if I got stuck paying the check?" —Ozzie

It was fun to watch guys like Terry and Vince develop. They were so full of energy and so excited to be in the big leagues that they were soaking in everything. Willie worked well with them, too. Vince even moved in with Willie for a while, kind of reversing the roles from when Willie had stayed with me. Both those guys asked a lot of questions, and I think their enthusiasm rubbed off on everybody on the team.

The one big change we had in 1985 was in the bullpen. Bruce Sutter had signed with Atlanta as a free agent because the Cardinals would not give him a no-trade clause, so we had to find a new closer. Whitey did a great job of running a "bullpen by committee" for most of the season. We brought up Todd Worrell from the minors for the last month, and he took over the job and pitched great.

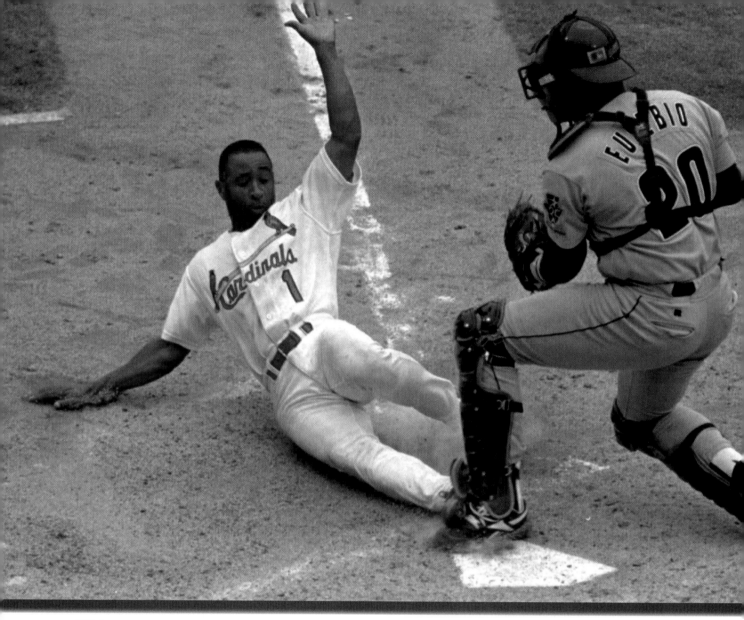

"This turned out to be the last time I scored, giving us a Labor Day win over the Astros in 1996. I scored from second on a hit by Willie McGee." –Ozzie
(AP Photo/Mary Butkus)

Knowing how to handle his relievers was one of Whitey's great strengths as a manager. Along with being able to communicate well with all of his players, handling his bullpen might be the most important job a manager has. You win or lose more games in late innings because of the matchups between a hitter and a reliever, and a manager who gets the right matchups the majority of the time is the one who is going to be successful. It goes right back to Whitey's basic strategy of putting all of his players in the position where they have the greatest chance to be successful, and it was no different when it came to putting relievers in the game.

Cincinnati Reds shortstop Barry Larkin, left, prepares to hug Ozzie during ceremonies honoring Smith's retirement, Saturday, Sept. 28, 1996, at Busch Stadium in St. Louis.(AP Photo/Mary Butkus)

"As is often the case in baseball, however, I found out that repeating as champion is not easy."

Ozzie watches his team get shut out by the Atlanta Braves 14-0 in Game 5 of the National League Championship Series Monday, Oct. 14, 1996, at Busch Stadium in St. Louis. This was Smith's last appearance at home. (AP Photo/Beth A. Keiser)

Communication is so important between a manager and his players. A player doesn't have to love his manager, but he does have to respect him and his knowledge of the game. A lot of today's managers are former players, because today's players won't listen to or respect a manager who didn't play the game. "What does he know?" they scoff. Well, he could know a lot if they would sit down and listen.

Whitey was always talking to his players. A lot of the guys went fishing with him over in Illinois during the morning. I wasn't much of a fisherman, but we had our chances to talk too. Whitey always cared about you and your family, and he treated everybody as if they were family. He spent as much time talking to our backup players as he did the starters, and that kept everybody positive, knowing that the manager knew who they were and that he considered them an important part of his team.

Whitey always kept his bench guys prepared and ready to play. He was so good at predicting what was going to happen in a game that two or three innings ahead of time he would tell a guy to get ready, because he would be hitting against so-and-so in the seventh or eighth inning, and darned if it didn't happen that way almost all of the time. Guys could prepare adequately because they knew their role and how they were going to be used. That's the same way he handled the pitchers in the bullpen.

When you are on a winning team, there is no better place to be than at the ballpark. Everybody is relaxed, having a good time, and we had such a good bunch of guys on all of the teams I played with that it really didn't seem like work most of the time. Whitey really only had two rules—be on time and give 100 percent—and as long as you did that, nobody had any problems.

One thing that happened to me in 1985 impacted me for the rest of my career, but nobody knew about it. That was the season I tore the rotator cuff in my right shoulder. I had hurt my shoulder diving into first base, and when I tried to compensate for that injury by changing the angle of my throws, I ended up tearing my rotator cuff.

I didn't tell anybody about the injury, because I wanted to keep playing and didn't want anybody thinking they could run on me or take advantage of the injury. I tried to do almost everything except throw a baseball left-handed—opening a door, turning on the radio, everything. It didn't get any better, but it was good enough that I didn't have to have surgery, and I was able to make enough adjustments in either positioning or the angle of my throws that the injury really didn't affect us too much.

"Dressing well has always been important to me, almost as important as baseball."
—Ozzie

We were locked in a great pennant race with the Mets, and our rivalry with them in the mid-1980s was something special. The greatest rival of the Cardinals will always be the Cubs, but rarely did we ever play Chicago when first place was on the line. And the Mets had some great players, like Darryl Strawberry and Doc Gooden.

The season came down to the final week, and we had a three-game lead over the Mets as they came to St. Louis. The Mets had to sweep us to tie, and we knew that even if we won only one game, we would be in first place when they left town.

The first night, the air was crisp, Busch Stadium was packed, and the game had all the atmosphere of a playoff game. Tudor battled Ron Darling, and the game was scoreless into the 11th inning. Then Strawberry hit a pitch from Ken Dayley off the scoreboard clock, and the Mets had won the opener, 1-0.

The pitching matchup the next day was almost as good, Joaquin Andujar against Gooden, and Gooden won, 5-2. Our lead was down to one game with one game left against the Mets and four games to go in the regular season.

Danny Cox started the final game of the series for us, and he came through with a 4-3 win. We were back up by two games with four to play, and we clinched the title two days later. Willie was named the league's MVP, Vince won the Rookie of the Year award, Tudor and Andujar each won 20 games, and it really was a great team.

We moved on to play the Dodgers in the playoffs and promptly lost the first two games in Los Angeles. The plane ride home was long and quiet, but I don't think anybody thought we were done. All we had to do was win a couple of games to get the series even again, then take our chances. We won the third game and were preparing for game four when one of those strange and unpredictable events occurred.

We were just completing batting practice when it began to rain. Busch Stadium still had artificial turf at the time, and they used a big, heavy, electric tarpaulin. As everybody was tossing their equipment into the dugout, the grounds crew started to roll out the tarp. Vince had his back turned and didn't see the tarp. He got his leg caught, and the tarp started to roll over him.

It was really one of the scariest things I had ever seen on the baseball field. People started yelling, trying to get the attention of the guy controlling the tarp. He was way out beyond first base, and Vince was near the plate. Finally the guy heard all the screaming and stopped the tarp after it had almost reached Vince's waist. Then, to get the tarp off him, they had to roll it back the other way, going over his leg again.

We carried Vince into the training room. He was in a lot of pain, but luckily we found out he had not been seriously hurt. He had suffered a chip fracture, which although not very serious did knock him out for the rest of the year. Everybody picked up their game a little to compensate for Vince being out, and we bombed the Dodgers to even the series.

Game five is always a critical game. I don't know the statistics, but I am certain the team that wins the fifth game of a tied series almost always goes on to win the series. We knew how important the game was, especially because we would be playing game six, and if necessary game seven, in Los Angeles. We were tied 2-2 going to the bottom of the ninth.

What happened next is probably the single most replayed highlight of my career. It is kind of funny that people consider me a defensive player, but the first thing I hear about when I am introduced to somebody is almost always where they were or what they were doing when I came up to bat against Tom Niedenfuer.

For the first time in my professional career, I hit a home run batting left-handed. It just got over the right field wall, but it counted the same as a blast that went 400 feet. We had won the game and now led the series 3-2.

One of the reasons that home run is replayed so often is the call Jack Buck made on the radio to describe the homer. He told people, "Go crazy, folks, go crazy, it's a home run, and the Cardinals have won the game, 3-2, on a home run by the Wizard." Because it was a day game, many people were just getting off work at that point in the game and were in their cars, listening on the radio as they were driving home. As soon as Jack told them what happened, they started honking their horns and basically going crazy.

A moment like that is always special and stands out as a highlight for the rest of your career. I remember telling reporters after the game that what I really hoped would occur because of the home run was that people would give me a little more credit for being a good offensive player. I was certainly never going to be a guy who hit a lot of home runs, and I was always going to have my detractors, but if that homer convinced a few people to take me a little more seriously as a multidimensional player, I would be happy.

The biggest reason I was happy, of course, was that we had won the game and were now going back to Los Angeles with two chances to win one game. None of us wanted to play a seventh game, however, and Jack Clark took care of that with a homer of his own in the ninth inning of game six. We had reached the World Series again.

Our opponents this time were the Kansas City Royals, our cross-state rivals and Whitey's former team. We played them in spring training, but this was in the days before interleague play, so we had never faced them in the regular season.

We definitely wanted to win, and we got off to a good start by winning the first two games in Kansas City. The Royals responded by winning two of the three games in St. Louis, but we were up 3-2 going back to Kansas City for game six.

What happened that night has been replayed on television almost as many times as my homer. We were three outs away from winning the championship when the Royals came up to bat in the bottom of the ninth, losing 1-0. Jorge Orta hit a slow roller to first.

St. Louis Cardinals fans watch the Cubs-Cardinals game at Busch Stadium in St. Louis, Sept. 17, 1996. (AP Photo/James A. Finley)

Clark got the ball and flipped it to Todd Worrell, who was running toward the base. Almost unbelievably, umpire Don Denkinger called Orta safe. Worrell clearly beat Orta to the base, but that wasn't the way Denkinger called it. Everybody argued, and the replays showed Orta was out, but Denkinger wasn't going to change his call.

That gave the Royals a chance, and they scored two runs and won the game 2-1. All everybody on our side could talk about after the game was the missed call, and mentally, we were done even before we took the field for game seven. It wasn't long before we were done physically, too, as we got bombed 11-0. Whitey and Andujar got kicked out of the game by Denkinger, who as luck would have it was working behind the plate for that game.

Ozzie reacts to his ninth-inning game-winning home run Oct.15, 1985. The Cardinals defeated the Los Angeles Dodgers 3-2 for a one-game advantage in the National League Playoffs. (AP PHOTO)

The bitter taste of that game and losing the series lasted for a long time. You tell yourself to forget it and get over it, but that is easier said than done. I think we were still thinking about it, and feeling somewhat sorry for ourselves, when we reported to spring training the next year. I am not going to place the entire blame for our bad season on the carry-over effect of those last two games, but I do think it was a factor. We were 24 games behind the Mets by the All-Star break, and they coasted to the pennant.

Losing like that gave us a little better focus as we prepared for the 1987 season, and I personally was determined to become better. A friend hooked me up with Mackie Shilstone, a physical trainer in New Orleans. He designed a program to make me stronger and enable me to keep a heftier weight throughout the season, which I thought would make me a better player. The results were even better than I had hoped or expected.

At the All-Star break, my average was at .301. I really wanted to hit .300 for the full year, because that is one of those magical numbers in baseball. Everybody's goal is to be a .300 hitter, and if you can do that, you have earned a place as one of the better hitters in the game. I really was determined to do it, especially since my offensive ability had been so much maligned over the years.

We had another spirited pennant race with the Mets and came out on top again. I also met my goal, finishing the year with a .303 average and a career-high 75 RBI. I was proud of that accomplishment because I knew how hard I had worked to achieve it. As happy as I was to hit .300, I think I was more proud of the 75 RBI. I had hit second all year, and because Vince was on base so often, I had a chance to drive in those runs. Scoring runs is how you win games, so there is no way you can underestimate the importance of RBIs.

There was quite a bit of talk in the media about whether I should win the league's Most Valuable Player award. There is a gray area about the award, which is voted on by the writers. The word *valuable* can be pretty tricky when you go to write the definition.

Ozzie Smith peeks out from behind his glove and leaps over Chicago Cubs' Mark Grace after completing the first half of a double play in the sixth inning, Thursday, Sept. 19, 1996, at Busch Stadium in St. Louis. (AP Photo/Mary Butkus)

The award isn't for the *best* player in the league, it's the *most valuable*. Even though the Cubs finished in last place, Andre Dawson won the MVP award. I finished second. Andre Dawson is a great player and had had a great year, but some people asked, "How valuable was he if the Cubs finished last even with him having that kind of year?" Where would they have finished without him?

My sole determination at that point was to beat the Giants and get back to the World Series. We had developed a nice little rivalry with San Francisco because they had some very spirited players over there, guys like Will Clark and Jeffrey Leonard. It was a good series, and we won to reach the World Series for the third time in six seasons.

The Minnesota Twins won the American League title, and because of the rotation of the home field advantage, we opened the World Series at the Metrodome. I had been there once before, for the 1985 All-Star game, and I didn't think it was a very good place to play baseball. The roof is strange, and it is hard to pick up the balls on popups. There is a big baggy wall in right field, and some of the air currents seemed to go on and off at different times.

We lost the first two games then came home and won three straight, but we didn't have the same feeling going back to Minnesota up 3-2 as we had going back to Kansas City two years earlier. I really don't think we were that confident we were going to win, and we didn't. The Twins won games six and seven to become world champions.

We were disappointed, but at least we had not been embarrassed as we had against the Royals. We had played the series without two of our regulars, Clark and Pendleton, who were hurt, and that had made a big difference.

That season, I was most proud of my offensive improvement, and other people had noticed it. Considering where I had come from, and how poor of a hitter I was when I first reached the major leagues, to get to .300 with 75 RBI was a very proud moment for me. I learned that the keys to being offensively successful were developing discipline at the plate, laying off bad pitches, learning to hit strikes, and having an idea before every at-bat as to what it was I was trying to accomplish in that particular time at the plate.

I know I was blessed with a lot of physical skills, but one thing I am very proud of in my career is that I never took anything for granted. I worked at developing my skills, and I worked to be the best player I could be. I knew I could do it, and I wanted to do it, and I wasn't going to accept not trying to make myself the best player I could be. Baseball is littered with players who had far greater ability than me and wasted it through lack of effort. My goal every day and every game was to give the greatest effort possible. Was I always successful? No. But I can assure everyone it was not for lack of trying.

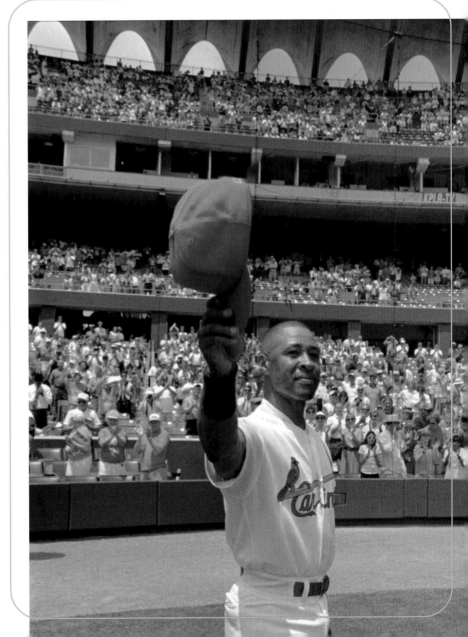

Ozzie waves to fans prior to the Cardinals game against the Philadelphia Phillies at Busch Stadium in St. Louis Wednesday, June 19, 1996. Smith announced that he would retire as an active player following the 1996 baseball season. Cardinals officials announced that his jersey would be retired. (AP Photo/Mary Butkus)

It was always exciting for me to go into the away ballparks and be recognized and cheered by the fans. The fans in St. Louis are like that, too, with visiting players. They want the Cardinals to win, and they are cheering hard for them, but they appreciate and value the great players on other teams. It was an honor for me when Whitey commented that he knew people in other towns were coming to the games because they wanted to see me play.

I didn't ever want to cheat anybody or give less than my best effort. And I can honestly say that if I asked myself after every game of my career if I had given my best effort and tried my hardest, the answer would be yes. That was the only way I knew how to play.

Ozzie wears a Schottzie hat presented to him by Reds owner Marge Schott, left, as they pose with Cincinnati Reds shortstop Barry Larkin, right, Friday, Sept. 20, 1996, at ceremonies honoring Smith in Cincinnati. (AP Photo/Al Behrman)

The 1987 season was my 10th year in the major leagues, a milestone for any player. I didn't know how much longer I wanted to play, but I knew I still loved the game and competing and coming to the ballpark every day. What I didn't know then was that I had played in my last World Series.

In any sport you can only keep a good team together for a few years. You have to make changes, and if those changes work out well, a team can continue winning. Those changes don't always work, however, and that is what happened to the Cardinals.

"Pedro Guerrero, myself and Vince Coleman were always laughing at somebody or something." –Ozzie

Ozzie acknowledges the fans while Ray Lankford, right, congratulates teammate Willie McGee after McGee singled in the 10th inning to defeat the Houston Astros 8-7, Monday, Sept. 2, 1996, at Busch Stadium in St. Louis. (AP Photo/Leon Algee)

"I know I was blessed with a lot of physical skills, but one thing I am very proud of in my career is that I never took anything for granted."

Before we knew it, it seemed like we had a bunch of new players. Jack Clark left, Vince Coleman left, Willie was traded, Terry Pendleton left. Finally, the biggest change occurred when Whitey got frustrated and resigned. We were struggling on the field, and unfortunately, when Mr. Busch passed away, a lot of the fun seemed to go out of the game for Whitey.

We had a few chances to win over the next few years but couldn't quite get it done. We changed owners, we changed general managers, we changed managers, we changed players, but we still came up short.

Ozzie is congratulated by David Bell (27) and other teammates for a defensive play in the seventh inning against the Philadelphia Phillies at Al Lang Stadium in St. Petersburg, Fla., Wednesday, March 20, 1996. (AP Photo/James A. Finley)

Ozzie tips his batting helmet to the cheers of the crowd at Atlanta-Fulton County Stadium after his at-bat in the sixth inning of Game 7 of the National League Championship Series in Atlanta Thursday, Oct. 17, 1996. (AP Photo/Elise Amendola)

ST. LOUIS will always be the LAND of OZ

"I could not have been happier playing for all the great fans in St. Louis." –Ozzie

One thing that didn't change was our fans. Opposing players always used to come up to me when they were on base, or when I would get on base, and tell me how lucky I was to play in St. Louis. If you took a poll of the players around the league and asked them, if they had to change teams, what city would they most like to move to, I think the easy winner would be St. Louis.

There is a reason I have made my permanent home in St. Louis for the last 20 years, and that is the people. The people of St. Louis, not just the fans who come out to the ballpark in record numbers every year, are the reason St. Louis is such a great baseball town. These people understand and appreciate hard work, and they want to love their players. They don't want to hate them and call them derogatory names. They want to cheer for them, and love them, and rejoice in their success. You don't find that in a lot of towns. When we broke attendance records year after year, even in seasons when we didn't win the pennant, it was very rewarding and meaningful. I can tell you it is much more fun to play in front of 40,000 people per night than in front of 5,000. Baseball players, like all professional athletes, are entertainers, and playing to a packed house always provides you that little extra energy you need to try even harder.

"My kids always enjoyed Fredbird, the Cardinal mascot." –Ozzie

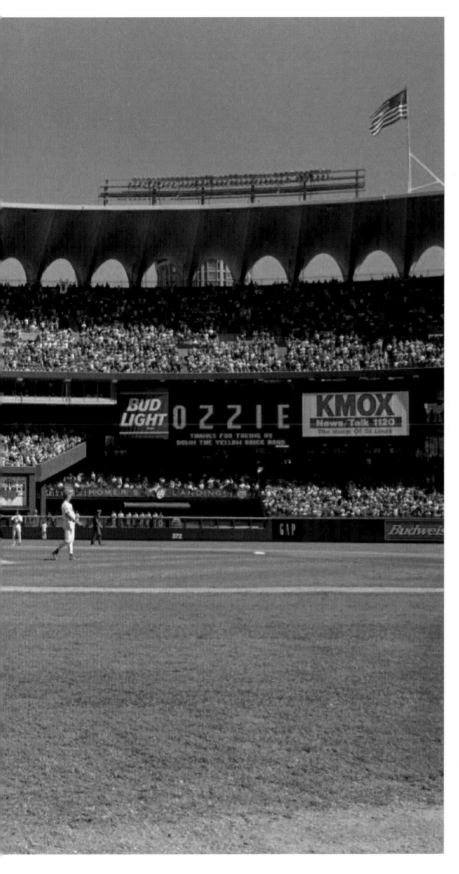

"It's a really good feeling when people say things like 'You are the reason I watch baseball, that I got involved, and I want my son to be like you.'"

Ozzie waves to the crowd of 51,379 fans at the Cincinnati Reds-Cardinals game, as he leaves the field for the last time during a regular season game, Sunday, Sept. 29, 1996, at Busch Stadium in St. Louis. Smith would retire after this season. (AP Photo/Mary Butkus)

"I wish more players understood the history of the game, especially how the Negro League players suffered to make a place in this game for future generations." –Ozzie

"There is a reason I have made my permanent home in St. Louis for the last 20 years, and that is the people."

Unfortunately, I think there are far too many players who take the fans for granted, not just in St. Louis but in all cities. Everybody who wears a major league uniform is incredibly lucky and should thank God every day for that opportunity. Too many of them don't, and those are the ones who have trouble when it comes to recognizing and appreciating the fans and getting involved with activities in the community.

There have been times when I physically did not have time to sign all of the autographs for fans who waited after games or in the hotel lobbies. But I signed as many as I could. I don't understand players who won't sign autographs. Don't they remember when they were young boys and major league players were like gods to them? What would they have given to get one of their heroe's autographs on a piece of paper?

"The end of a career. I wish I could have played a little longer, but I really have no regrets." –Ozzie

It really rubs me the wrong way when I see players walk right past a group of fans, especially kids, without stopping to sign or at least acknowledge the people who are waiting there. Baseball players have to honor and respect the fans—they are the reason we have an audience.

That's the same reason why I have chosen to be so active in the St. Louis community through organizations and charity work. It is a way I can give something back to the community and to the fans who have supported me all of the years of my career. There are only 24 hours in a day, and I do get more requests for time and contributions than are physically possible in one day, but I try to do as much as I can. It is my small attempt to tell all of these people "thank you."

When I made the decision to retire in 1996, I felt I was physically still capable of playing for a couple more years. All of the work I had done to strengthen my body had enabled me to not get run down at the end of the year, and I felt I could still make a positive contribution, especially to a winning club. Unfortunately, it became obvious to me that I was not wanted by the new regime which had taken over the Cardinals.

I probably could have signed with one of a couple of other teams to continue my career, but I didn't want to do that. I was a Cardinal, I am a Cardinal, and I think too much of the people in St. Louis to have them see me finishing my career wearing a different uniform.

Knowing when to quit and deciding how to walk away from a game you have played all of your life are tough for any athlete. Sometimes, because of an injury, you have no choice. Sometimes the club decides for you. Even though I knew in my heart I could still play, I didn't want to be one of those players who hang on for a few more years by bouncing from team to team, just because they don't know what else they are going to do with their lives after they stop playing their sport. I played 19 years in the major leagues, and it was time to go out gracefully and say my thank-yous and goodbyes.

"Thanks for the memories."
—Ozzie

Ozzie acknowledges the crowd as they give him a standing ovation in the first inning against the Cincinnati Reds Sunday, Sept. 29, 1996. (AP Photo/Mary Butkus)

Saying "thank you" is a virtually impossible task. You start naming names, you forget somebody, and feelings are hurt. There is no doubt, however, that I owe my success to a lot of people who have helped me along the way. Alvin Dark believed in me even though I had only played 68 games in a low minor league, and he made me the Padres' starting shortstop as a rookie. Whitey Herzog brought me to St. Louis and helped me become a better player. All of my San Diego and St. Louis coaches and teammates each helped me in different ways. The fans also played a tremendous role in my success.

Ozzie celebrates his team's clinching of the National League Central Division title after beating the Pirates in Pittsburgh 7-1 on Tuesday, Sept. 24, 1996. ``To look in Ozzie Smith's eyes and see how happy he is, to win this in his last season, makes it real special," Cardinals starter Andy Benes said. ``It's a great night for the Cardinals."(AP Photo/Gary Tramontina)

"I wanted people to respect me the way I respected the game."

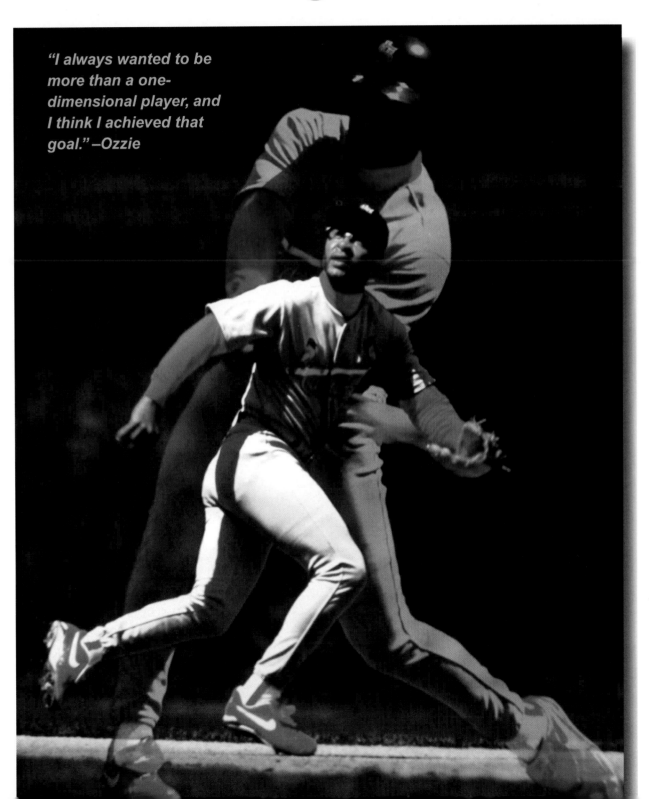

"I always wanted to be more than a one-dimensional player, and I think I achieved that goal." –Ozzie

"Saying 'thank you' is a virtually impossible task."

Ozzie tearfully announces he is retiring from baseball during a press conference, June 19, 1996. Smith was elected to the Baseball Hall of Fame by a margin of 93 percent and is the only member of this year's class. (Bill Greenblatt, UPI)

Alvin Dark told me that I was going to be a great player and that all I had to do was go out and catch the ball and throw it across the infield. He was right.

People always talk about the great plays I made during my career, but I think I am more proud of all the routine plays that I made. Baseball is not a series of highlights strung together for the 10 p.m. news. It is 162 games, spread over six months, preceded by spring training and followed by the playoffs and World Series, if you are lucky enough to get there. You have far more routine plays than great plays in a season and in a career, and how you performed on those plays is far more important to your personal and team success than making a few diving stops which become highlight material.

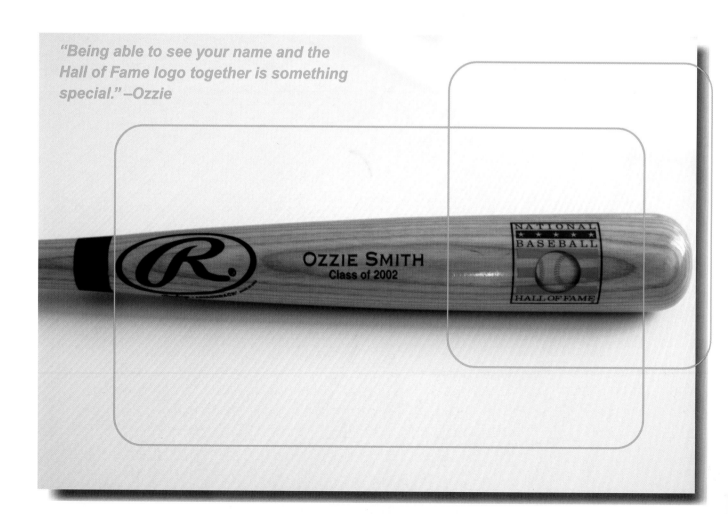

"Being able to see your name and the Hall of Fame logo together is something special." —Ozzie

Anybody can make a great play now and then. What I did, I did every day.

I was able to achieve a great deal in my career, capped by induction into the Hall of Fame. I was able to set some records and achieve some great personal milestones, such as the night in 1992 when I recorded my 2,000th hit in the major leagues.

A friend of mine came up to me and said, "Do you know you are close to 2,000 hits?" I told him to get lost. He persisted, telling me to look at the back of my baseball card. When I did, I saw I was only 40 hits away from 2,000 career hits. When I did get that hit, I think it validated everything I was trying to accomplish in my career. I don't know too many one-dimensional defensive players who get almost 2,500 hits in their careers.

"Fans have made and sent me some special items over the years, including this needlepoint which commemorates my 2,000th hit." —Ozzie

Top: Ozzie acknowledges fans during his retirement ceremony, Saturday, Sept. 28, 1996, at Busch Stadium in St. Louis. At right is Smith's son, O.J. (AP Photo/Leon Algee)

Bottom: Ozzie and Willie McGee laugh at teammate Vince Coleman during Willie McGee Day before the game against the Milwaukee Brewers, Sunday, April 9, 2000, at Busch Stadium in St. Louis. McGee retired this year.(AP Photo/Mary Butkus)

I have the record for most assists in a season. I have the record for fewest errors in a season by a shortstop. I have the career records for most double-plays and most assists. I won 13 consecutive Gold Gloves. I went to 15 All-Star games. I took pride in knowing so many people came out to watch me play, and I never wanted them to go home disappointed.

Wearing the Padres' and then the Cardinals' uniform was an honor for me. I was proud to be a major leaguer. I wanted to carry myself with dignity. I wanted people to respect me the way I respected the game. I made a commitment to be the best player I could be, and that was my single driving goal every day of my career.

"I am surrounded by some of my favorite things." —Ozzie

Ozzie waves to the fans at Busch Stadium prior to making the ceremonial first pitch before the Cardinals' seasonal opener against the Colorado Rockies Monday, April 1, 2002. (AP Photo/James A. Finley)

Fans have to understand that players are human too. We aren't perfect; we are going to make mistakes. We are not going to get a hit every time we come up to bat in a critical situation. We are going to make defensive errors. Our team is not always going to win the World Series.

I think the fans know and understand that. I also think they understand when a player is giving everything he has to the game, that he is trying just as hard as they would try if they were in his position.

"Collecting bobblehead dolls is a big craze now and I have mine as well." –Ozzie

I was always told I was too small, but I never accepted that. If you pursue excellence, you can achieve it, regardless of your size.

Because I was not a physically intimidating player, I think fans might have identified with me a little more than with some other players. What I really wanted from them, however, was the acknowledgement that everything I did, every game I played, was done with 100 percent effort. I was working hard to achieve big things, exactly what I would have expected of the players I cheered for as a fan. Fans deserve nothing less.

Ozzie watches the crowd give him a standing ovation in the seventh inning of the All-Star Game Tuesday, July 9, 1996, in Philadelphia's Veterans Stadium. This was the last All-Star Game for Smith who announced his retirement earlier that season. (AP Photo/Rusty Kennedy)

"How do you want to be remembered?"

"I think it's always been my goal to be respected for the way that I went about

my business. I always wanted to project a very professional manner when I represented

myself, the club, and major league baseball. I think for the most part when people

comment or when they see me out on the street, one

of the phrases that I hear a lot

Ozzie tips his hat to baseball fans during a ceremony honoring the retiring shortstop before the game with the Pittsburgh Pirates in Pittsburgh on Tuesday, Sept. 24, 1996.
(AP Photo/Gene J. Puskar)

is "class act." That is a very good way to be remembered, as a class act, someone who always handled himself in a professional manner. That was always important to me and my reputation. I realize the importance that we as athletes have as role models for kids. Being a parent really brings that to the forefront, teaching patience and reminding us how influential we are as far as kids are concerned. I want to be remembered as a person who was caring, very thoughtful and very professional in the way he went about his business.

"If I go by what people tell me on the street, it's a really good feeling when people say things like, 'You are the reason I watch baseball, that I got involved, and I want my son to be like you.' That's quite a compliment."

"It is always nice to have the things you do appreciated by others." —Ozzie

"What is your greatest accomplishment?"

"Making the Hall of Fame is great, but as an athlete that wasn't something that I set out to do. I set out to be the very best that I could be with what I was given. The Hall of Fame became kind of a by-product of working hard to be as consistent as I could possibly be and to be the very best that I could be. When you look at all the Hall of Famers, the one thing they probably have in common is that their one goal was to work hard and be the best they could be. You don't want to ever leave the game and feel you left something out there or that you took something for granted.

"A Hall of Fame jersey is a treasure for any player." –Ozzie

"My greatest accomplishment is something that probably would surprise a lot of people. They always think of a big offensive play or a big defensive play. The home run in 1985 was big, because it gave us life and enabled us to go on to the World Series. But my greatest accomplishment as an athlete had to be playing from 1985 to 1996 at a very high level with a torn rotator cuff. What happens as you get older and as you slow down is that people say you lost a step here or there. You don't do things at age 36 the way you did at 26. There was always a saying that "He was 10 steps ahead," and you come back the next year and they say "he's lost a step." What that means to me is that I am still nine steps ahead. When I was told I had a torn

"Some of the awards I have won over the years stand out, such as the Branch Rickey Award for humanitarian service." —Ozzie

rotator cuff, I remember sitting on the edge of the bed crying because I knew that it could be career-threatening, and not knowing whether I was going to be able to bounce back. It happened just before the All-Star game in 1985. We were playing the Padres, and I dove into first base and jammed my shoulder. That was when the impingement started, and because I played every day it just got progressively worse. The only way I was going to help my team was by being on the field. I don't think there are any players who go out there 100 percent, no aches and pains anywhere. I was no different. There were many days that I went out there when I didn't feel like being out there, but I knew it meant more for me to be out there for my team. Winning is much more than just getting a big hit or making a big play. It's being able to help your team psychologically.

"I was worried, because I knew Rick Burleson had a torn rotator cuff, and I knew how hard he worked without ever being able to really come back. I didn't want to have surgery. Through my work with a trainer, Mackie Shilstone, I was able to protect the area around the tear and get a lot more mileage out of playing with a torn rotator cuff.

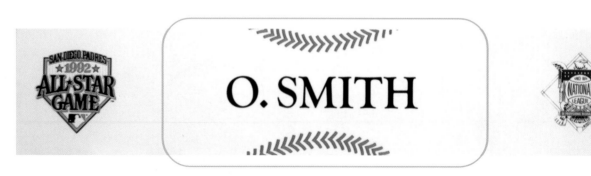

"Being named to an All-Star team was an honor I always appreciated." –Ozzie

The only surgery that I had was to shave the bone down in my shoulder, and that was

arthroscopic. It allowed me to get back on top of throwing again because of all the other

rehab I had done. When I retired in 1996, I was probably throwing the ball as well as I had

in the last 10 years. "

Ozzie tries to throw side-armed to first base after forcing out Atlanta Braves base runner Mark Lemke after a Chipper Jones ground ball during the third inning in Atlanta, Monday, June 24, 1996.
(AP Photo/John Bazemore)

Who were your heroes?

"I don't know if I had any heroes. There were people whom I enjoyed watching. I enjoyed watching Roberto Clemente play. I liked his style. I grew up as a Los Angeles Dodgers fan, and I would catch the bus from south central LA out to Dodger Stadium, sit in the bleachers with all of the other bleacher bums, and try to catch home runs during batting practice. I would watch those major leaguers catching fly balls behind their backs, and things like that were always fascinating to me. Then one day I found myself in the big leagues doing the same thing and wondering if there were young Ozzie Smiths sitting there watching me, doing the same thing I did.

"I didn't really pattern myself after anybody, because I realized at a young age that everybody is different. You have to do things the way they are the most comfortable for you. That was what I always tried to do. People ask me about diving; that was just me, that was how I did it. It was one of the things that became kind of a trademark."

"It's a good thing I was doing the punching in this moment I spent with Muhammad Ali." –Ozzie

What were the keys to your success?

"It's pretty simple. You work hard. Perseverance, dedication, courage, the intestinal fortitude to be the best you can be, those are the keys not only to my success but to anybody's. You've got to be willing to go the extra mile. You've got to be willing to sacrifice. There has to be some blood, some sweat and some tears. There's no success without them. That is really the key: being able to put your head in there and grind it out. Every day is not going to be a great day. Having that desire

"Winning a Gold Glove was and is a special achievement."
—Ozzie

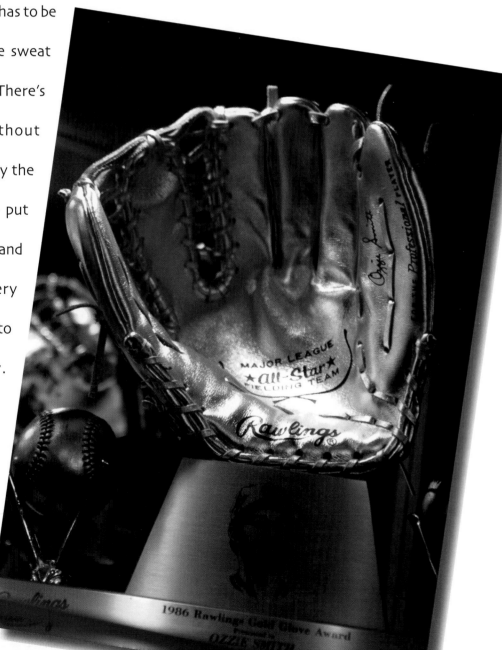

to grind and work through your problems and learn from them is what being successful is all about.

"From a talent standpoint, most people are pretty even. The things that make the difference are the consistency with which you play and your drive and determination to be the very best that you can be. Those are my goal. When I talk with other people about what it was that made them go, it's pretty much the same thing. They were afraid of failure. Being afraid to fail drives you even more than being successful. I was afraid of failure, but failure is part of success. It's how you handle it that is the most important thing. Failure on the baseball field should be used as a learning tool. I wanted to succeed more than I wanted to fail. I know the feeling of failure did not rival the feeling of being successful. I wanted to experience success a lot more than I wanted to experience failure. I knew it was going to take a little extra if I was going to be better than the next guy. One thing I always told my teammates was that some days when you go out on the field, there will be people who are more talented. Some days when you go out on the field there are going to be people who are smarter. As a player, you cannot let him have both of those things. If you can't out-play him, you'd better be able to out-think him. If you can't out-think him, you'd better be able to out-play him."

"You've got to be willing to go the extra mile. You've got to be willing to sacrifice."

What are your favorite defensive plays?

"The Jeff Burroughs play is still at the top. I had been in the major leagues for less than a month. We were playing the Braves in San Diego, and Jeff Burroughs hit a ball up the middle that looked as if it was going to go into center field. I dove to try to get it. As I dove, the ball took a bad hop and started to go over my head. I threw up my bare hand and caught the ball. I scrambled to my feet and threw him out at first base.

"My greatest play as a Cardinal came against Von Hayes of the Pirates in 1986. Von hit a fly ball into short left field. Curt Ford was playing left, and he was running in and dove. I was going out and I dove. He went under me, and I went over the top of him and caught the ball. We could have slammed together, but luckily we avoided each other.

"The play going away with my back to the infield has always been one of my favorites. It takes so much, all the little intricate things that people don't see or know that you as a player have to be thinking about. I practiced that play a lot. Willie Mays made one of those; I made it a lot of times.

"A great defensive play just happens. You can practice going out and catching a ball over your shoulder or over your head, which I did all the time. Great plays are the thing that stands out in people's minds, but they are very reactionary. They stem from being in the right place at the right time, being around the ball. It was always a

"I prided myself on being able to change the momentum of a game with a great defensive play."

case of being in position to make a great play when the opportunity presented itself. People don't look at defense and consider that it can change the momentum of a game, but it can do that just as much as can an offensive play. I prided myself on being able to change the momentum of a game with a great defensive play."

"Sometimes you don't know how you caught a ball until you see the picture." –Ozzie

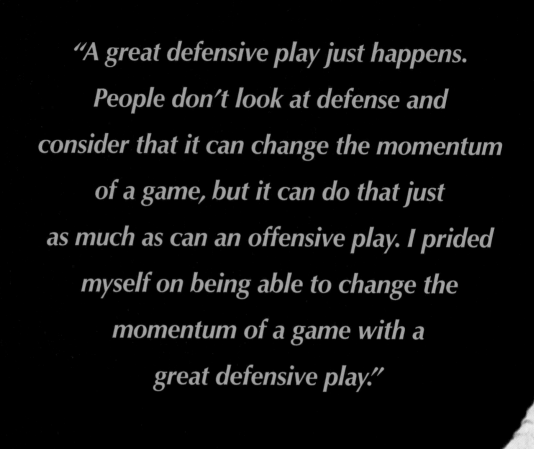

"A great defensive play just happens. People don't look at defense and consider that it can change the momentum of a game, but it can do that just as much as can an offensive play. I prided myself on being able to change the momentum of a game with a great defensive play."

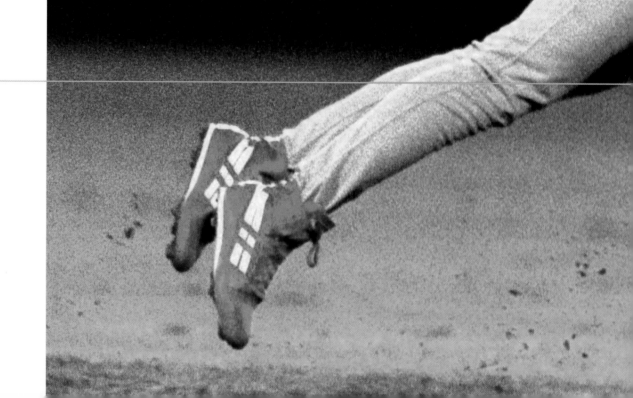

Ozzie leaps to catch a line drive in 1996. (John Kuntz, Reuters)

Will there ever be another Ozzie Smith?

"There will always be comparisons. We are all unique in going about what it is that we do. There will probably be someone who will come along and eclipse some of my records, but the things that I was able to do have allowed me to make it to the Hall of Fame. There's nothing more than that.

"The shortstop position has changed. The Cal Ripken style of shortstop is in vogue right now. Guys like Nomar Garciaparra in Boston, Alex Rodriguez in Texas and Derek Jeter in New York get all of the attention. There are guys I think are pretty good, but they get overlooked because those other guys are so offensively oriented. If you have guys hitting 50 home runs playing that position and playing pretty consistent defense, it's hard to overlook. I don't think that you could go wrong if you were going to start a ballclub by picking any one of those three guys. They are great players to build a team around. They are very good guys, and I respect them a lot. I think they respect me. They are holding the position very well."

Ozzie waves to the crowd at Busch Stadium in St. Louis on Wednesday, June 19, 1996, following the announcement that he was retiring as an active player with the team at the end of the 1996 season. (AP Photo/Mary Butkus)

How did the tradition of the backflips start?

"When I was a rookie with the Padres at spring training in 1978, we had to run a lot at the end of practice. We had to run a mile in a certain time and things like that. At the time I was young, and these old guys were there with their tongues hanging out. I wanted to show them that I wasn't tired, so at the end of the run I did a backflip. I had done flips all my life. I was a young kid who would try anything. I grew up across the street from a wood factory, and we used to go over there, put a plank between the stacks of wood, use that as a diving board, and flip into the sawdust. We used to take tire innertubes, have people sit on one side of them, and use them as springboards. We could get some height and flip that way. It turned out to be a great thing.

Ozzie flips in the air as he takes the field at the start of the third game of the National League Championship against the Los Angeles Dodgers in St. Louis in this Oct. 12, 1985 photo. (AP Photo/File)

"On the last day of the year, it was Fan Appreciation Day, and we had 50,000 people at the ballpark. We were not a very good team, and there was not much to cheer for, so we had to create some excitement. Andy Strasburg, our marketing guy, wanted me to do the flip, and Gene Tenace wanted me to do it. They each had a different agenda for the flip. Gene wanted me to do it to show his girls; Andy wanted me to do it to get the fans excited. I was a little reluctant to do it at first, because I didn't want to be tagged with the moniker of 'hot dog.' I did it, though, and it really got a lot of attention. Once I did it, it became a thing that

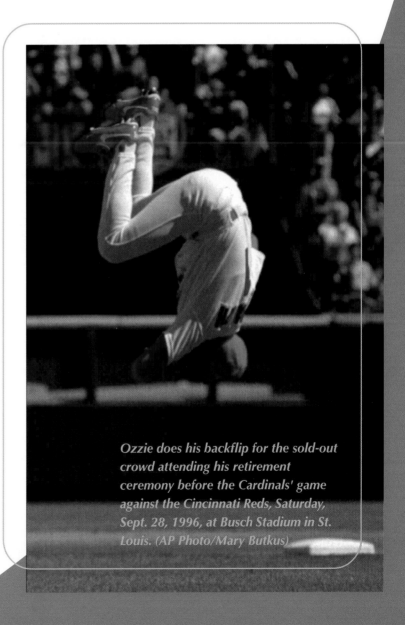

Ozzie does his backflip for the sold-out crowd attending his retirement ceremony before the Cardinals' game against the Cincinnati Reds, Saturday, Sept. 28, 1996, at Busch Stadium in St. Louis. (AP Photo/Mary Butkus)

"It takes another kind of talent to be able to complete a painting like this."
—Ozzie

people expected every year. To this day, people think it was something that I did every day, but that wasn't the case. I did it on the first day and the last day of the season, at home, and then later on for the big postseason games. It became a thing that people expected, especially in St. Louis. One year when I couldn't do it because of my shoulder injury, I had O.J., my son, who was 4 at the time, go out and flip, and the crowd loved it.

"I became famous for the flip, but I like people to know I did play a little baseball too. A lot of people come up to me now, and they may not remember the baseball, but they remember the flip. It's nice and I'm proud of it, but I want to be remembered for the consistent brand of baseball that I played, too."

"It's hard to tell who has the biggest smile, me or my son O.J."—Ozzie

"I became famous for the flip, but
I like people to know I did play a
little baseball too."

"The fans always enjoyed the flip, and I did too." –Ozzie

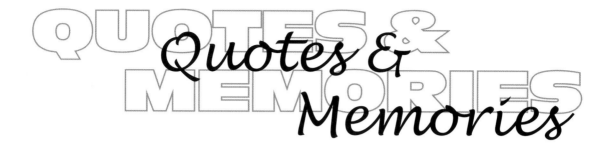

Quotes & Memories

QUOTES & MEMORIES

"I may be his teammate, but I'm also his fan. So many times I'll see a ball leaving the bat and say 'OK, that's a base hit.' And then somehow Ozzie will come up with it. A lot of the time I feel like standing out there and applauding with the rest of the fans. He's head and shoulders above every other shortstop."

– Former teammate Tom Herr, to **Sports Illustrated,** *in 1987*

" The thing about Ozzie is, if he misses a ball, you assume it's uncatchable. If any other shortstop misses a ball, your first thought is 'would Ozzie have had it?' "

– Former New York Mets manager Bud Harrelson,
to **Sports Illustrated,** *in 1987*

Ozzie throws to put out a Los Angeles Dodger in Los Angeles in this June 12, 1994 photo.
(AP Photo/Mark J. Terrill)

" The one word to best describe
Ozzie is 'spectacular.' Shortstops in the past
were never as conspicuous as Ozzie. In the old days
you had steady guys like Reese and Marion. You never
thought of them making the great play. They
were always just there in the right spot. But
Ozzie is an acrobat, and that makes him stand out. "

*– Dodgers broadcaster Vin Scully,
to* **Sports Illustrated,** *in 1987*

*Ozzie lines up a shot
during Kirby Puckett's
annual charity pool
tournament Saturday,
Nov. 17, 2001.
(AP Photo/Janet Hostetter)*

"Ozzie is spectacular. For one thing, he can dive for a ball and still get up in time to make the throw. But what he's done best for the position is make people in the game appreciate defense. In my day, unless you hit home runs, they didn't pay you anything. We defensive players were all underpaid. So I was glad to see Ozzie get his money. He's a crowd pleaser and the fans love him. He deserves it. What he's done is upgrade the glove."

– Former Cardinals shortstop Marty Marion, *to* **Sports Illustrated,** *in 1987*

Ozzie Smith, shown in this 1996 photo, winner of 13 Gold Gloves and regarded by many as the best defensive shortstop ever. (AP Photo/File)

"I saw him play for the first time in Little League,
and I played against him a few times in high school. You
could see he had ability. You can go back and ask anybody and they
will tell you the same thing. They were already calling
him the Wizard of Oz. He was amazing. He was no different
than he is now: balls couldn't go through."

– *Former Cardinals teammate Lonnie Smith*

*From left, St. Louis Cardinals great Lou Brock, Digger
Phelps, U.S. Postal Service CEO Clarence Lewis and
Ozzie Smith unveil the Legends of Baseball stamp series
prior to the Cardinals game against the Pittsburgh Pirates
Thursday, May 4, 2000 at Busch Stadium in St. Louis.
The new stamps honor 20 players from the last century.
(AP Photo/Tom Gannam)*

66 The one thing about Ozzie is that he really
worked on his hitting when he came from San Diego.
He was a .230, .240 hitter
when he got here and he worked at it over the years,
and he finally wound up at .260. There's no question
about it. He was a great credit to the game, he worked
hard, he played hard and he
took care of the fans. 99

– Former Cardinal and Hall of Famer Stan Musial

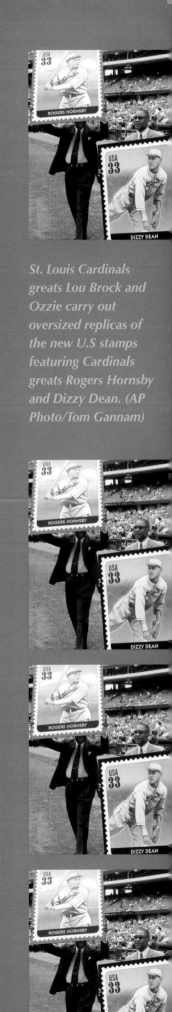

*St. Louis Cardinals
greats Lou Brock and
Ozzie carry out
oversized replicas of
the new U.S stamps
featuring Cardinals
greats Rogers Hornsby
and Dizzy Dean. (AP
Photo/Tom Gannam)*

" Here's a person who walked into the big leagues and was not really Hall of Fame material. He worked at it. I'm sure he had a lot of help along the way. "

— Former Cardinal and Hall of Famer Lou Brock

Former Cardinals and Hall of Famers Lou Brock, Ozzie Smith and Bob Gibson get together for a photograph before a game between the Cards and the San Diego Padres at Busch Stadium in St. Louis, Missouri, August 28, 2001. (Bill Greenblatt, UPI)

" He's the best defensive shortstop who ever played
the game. Ever. "

– Former San Francisco manager Roger Craig

" Ozzie shows what can happen when you make the most
out of your ability. He's a Hall of Famer whether
he has 2,000 hits or not. "

– Yankees and former Cardinals manager Joe Torre

"O.J. and Dustin, my two sons."–Ozzie

" Every player should have had the opportunity to be Ozzie Smith's teammate. Then you'd really find out how great this game can be, and more. "

– Former Cardinals teammate Jack Clark

"I enjoy spending time in the kitchen, both at home and at my two restaurants in St. Louis."
–Ozzie

"Not only was he a great defensive player, but he was a heck of a personality. Getting to know him, all that negativeness that had come over the years was gone. Right when I threw the pitch, they had a stat on the screen that he had never hit a home run left-handed. And then I was so stunned walking in [to the dugout], you'll notice that I almost ran into him rounding the bases.

"He was the start of making shortstop a glamour position. He's the one who changed the visual image in people's minds of a shortstop just picking up routine grounders and throwing to first. This guy was amazing."

– Former Dodgers pitcher Tom Niedenfuer, who gave up Smith's famous homer in the 1985 playoffs.

" Ozzie is such an outstanding ballplayer, but he's as great a person as he was a ballplayer in my eyes. Oz loves people and loves helping people. He wears his heart on his shoulder. It really shows. When I lived with him, I'd see him get up in the morning to go promote the game of baseball and the Cardinals. People didn't know how much he did that. That's what separates him from everyone else. He's a class act. "

– Former Cardinals teammate Willie McGee

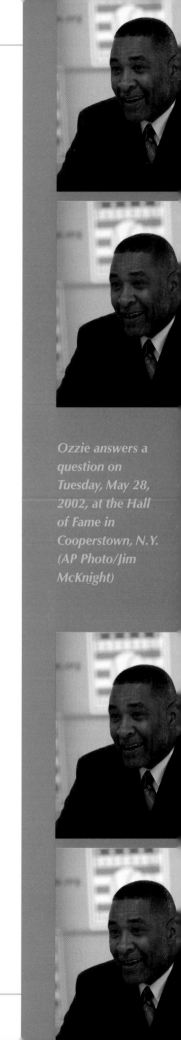

"Ozzie's great plays stand out in your mind. But what really stands out to me is that he didn't mess up the routine plays. He made all of those. His attention to detail, his pregame preparation, the focus he always had on the field. He never took for granted his skills as a defensive player. I don't think there will be another one like him. The Hall of Fame is for special players, and he fits into that category."

– *Former Cardinals teammate Tom Herr*

CHRISTOPHER S. BOND
MISSOURI

January 8, 2002

Ozzie - Congratulations on recieving the very well deserved recognition in the Hall of Fame. Good work! Have a wonderful 2002.

Rob

January 13, 2002

Dear Ozzie,

Please forgive the typewritten letter . Trust me, this will be easier to read than my long hand. 63 year old nerves affect your hands. I was thrilled for you when I saw the results of the HOF voting. If anybody needs verification of how you affected a game with your play, they can call me and I'll tell them I saw it in person.

I thoroughly enjoyed the brief time we played together and 1982 will always be my favorite season in baseball. I can still remember the fun times I had fielding ground balls with you during pre-game drills and even our time at Studio 54. By the way, when I went to a physical therapist in NY for some shoulder treatment, one of the therapists was Tito!. He has since left and I hope he's doing okay.

When I get my broadcast schedule finalized; I'm doing the Yankee games on the local NY network, I'm going to see if I can get to Cooperstown. I have been able to make it to the induction of most of my teammates, Killebrew, Carlton, Schmidt and now the "Wiz".

Hope you're healthy and happy and your family is doing well. It was a pleasure to play with you and I'm happy for you.

Sincerely,

Jim "Kitty" Kaat

ROBIN E. ROBERTS

NATIONAL BASEBALL HALL OF FAME
INDUCTED 1976

Dear Ozzie
Congratulations- a great honor. I heard a writer ask Dizzy Dean if he was The greatest pitcher that every lived. Dizzy thought a minute then answered "I'm not sure I was the best but I was amongst Them."

I'll answer for you Ozzie you were The best I ever saw -

See you in Cooperstown -

Again Congratulations Sincerely,
Robin Roberts

504 Terrace Hill Drive • Temple Terrace, Florida • 33617 • Fax (813)989-2976

PICKETT RAY & SILVER

Civil Engineers
Planners
Land Surveyors

333 Mid Rivers Mall Dr.
St. Peters, MO 63376
(314) 397-1211
Fax: (314) 397-1104

Richard C. Gunter
Golf Course Designer

OZZIE SMITH,

JAN. 24, 2002

CONGRATULATIONS ON YOUR INDUCTION INTO THE BASEBALL HALL OF FAME.

I DON'T KNOW ANYONE WHO WOULD NOT WANT THEIR SON OR DAUGHTER TO GROW UP TO BE LIKE YOU.

YOU ARE A ROLE MODEL, A CLASS ACT, AND ONE HECK OF A GIFTED ATHLETE.

IF THERE WOULD BE A HALL OF FAME FOR PEOPLE WHO ARE EXCEPTIONAL HUMAN BEINGS, YOU WOULD BE INDUCTED INTO THAT ON THE FIRST BALLOT ALSO.

BEST OF EVERYTHING IN THE FUTURE.

RICHARD C. GUNTER

DETROIT TIGERS

MAILING ADDRESS
P. O. BOX 70
SWIFTON, AR 72471

... y Congratulation —

Wow! — you Certainly
have seen most y the
I came to the majors
you were the best.

Beside being the best you are truly
a fine man. I suspect it has not all sunk
in yet — but you are joining a very Elite group.

I'm looking forward to seeing you
at the Induction.

Sincerely

George Kell

SALOMON SMITH BARNEY
A member of citigroup

Louis B. Susman
Vice Chairman
Global Corporate Investment Bank
Salomon Smith Barney Investment

January 11, 2002

Busch Stadium
250 Stadium Plaza
St. Louis, Missouri 63102

Attention: Mr. Ozzie Smith

Dear Ozzie:

Congratulations on the fantastic honor on being elected to the Baseball Hall of Fame.

I consider it one of my great contributions to St. Louis when we made the trade and signed you to your contract under my regime. I have not only been very proud of our professional relationship but our friendship that developed during that period.

Please let me know when your induction will be and I will try to make it and once again, congratulations.

Yours truly,

LBS/aar

Many good memories of our past — congratulations!

SALOMON SMITH BARNEY INC. 8700 Sears Tower, Chicago, IL 60606   FAX 312-876-8494

Jim Kaat　　　1/13/02

'Oz',
Congratulations! Well deserved and well earned. Hope I can be there for your special moment.
"Kitty"

Joseph A. McDonald
1057 Lake Hollingsworth Drive
Lakeland, Florida 33803

Dear Ozzie,

Working at Ebbets Field in my youth, I had the pleasure and privilege of seeing Reese, Marion, McMillan and many others play shortstop.

Your play and application of talent through dedication added a whole new dimension to the art of playing a most demanding position.

Thanks for the thrills and congratulations on a most worthy selection to the Hall of Fame.

Best always,

Joe McD

SOUTHWEST BANK OF ST. LOUIS
13205 MANCHESTER ROAD
SAINT LOUIS, MO. 63131

ANDREW N. BAUR
Chairman

January 25, 2002

Mr. Ozzie Smith

Dear Ozzie:

Congratulations on your election to the Hall of Fame. It is a great
honor for you, for the Cardinals and for St. Louis. To be elected on the
first ballot is perhaps the greatest honor a baseball player could ever
have. I know that Stan Musial always wears his Hall of Fame ring, as
he considers this the most important honor he has ever received.

Of course, long before I was an owner, I was a fan and you had no
bigger fan than the undersigned. Watching you play was one of the
great thrills of my life. I am looking forward to being in Cooperstown
for your Hall of Fame induction.

Congratulations and all the best wishes.

Sincerely,

Andrew N. Baur
Chairman

ANB:cbd

St. Louis Cardinals L.P.

Cardinals

Frederick O. Hanser
Chairman

Busch Stadium • 250 Stadium Plaza • St. Louis, MO • 63102-1722

January 23, 2002

Ozzie Smith

Dear Ozzie:

Congratulations again on your election to the National Baseball Hall of
Fame in Cooperstown, New York. What a wonderful crown to a fabulous
career. This recognition, which you so richly deserve, reflects many attributes
of your game, in addition to the standard of defense that you have set for all
players in the future. Your leadership, your success under pressure, your
career-long effort to improve your hitting, capped by your 300 season, and
your dedication to the high standards that you have set as a professional
baseball player.

The warm glow of your election spreads over all of us in baseball and
in particular, the St. Louis Cardinals. We look forward to a wonderful
induction ceremony in Cooperstown this July to celebrate your richly
deserved entry into that shrine. Thank you for bringing such credit to the
game of baseball and for all you have done for the St. Louis Cardinals and
their fans everywhere.

See you in Cooperstown.

With highest regards,

ST. LOUIS CARDINALS, L.P.

Frederick O. Hanser

FOH/gjh

World Champions • 1926 • 1931 • 1934 • 1942 • 1944 • 1946 • 1964 • 1967 • 1982

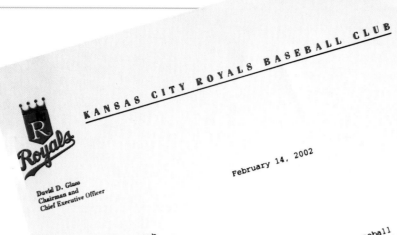

KANSAS CITY ROYALS BASEBALL CLUB

Royals

David D. Glass
Chairman and
Chief Executive Officer

February 14, 2002

Mr. Ozzie Smith

Dear Ozzie:

Congratulations on your recent election to the Baseball Hall of Fame! I cannot think of anyone more deserving of this recognition for what you brought to the game of baseball. Your legacy will long be remembered by the many fans who had the opportunity to watch you play and for others who read about the great things you did for the game over the years. Your work ethic, dedication and character has been an outstanding example for many of the young, upcoming players.

I am proud to say I had the opportunity to watch, Ozzie, the baseball player and to know Ozzie, the man. Thanks for giving the fans such thrills and setting the example for all of us.

On behalf of the entire Kansas City Royals Organization, please accept our congratulations for this well-deserved honor.

Sincerely,

David Glass

DDG:bkb

P.O. BOX 419969, Kansas City, Missouri 64141-6969 • 816-921-8000 • Fax 816-924-0347
1985 WORLD CHAMPIONS • 1980 AMERICAN LEAGUE CHAMPIONS • 1976-1977-1978-1984 AMERICAN LEAGUE WESTERN DIVISION CHAMPIONS

YOU'RE THE TALK OF THE TOWN!

1/10/02

Dear Ozzie,

Congratulations on your Selection into the Hall of Fame. During your 18 years with the Cardinals you brought much Joy to the Baseball fans of St. Louis, me and my Family included. Also to many Others, with your many charitable functions.

On three different occasions I had the Honor of playing Golf with you in the Whitey Herzog Tournaments.

I know you're going to be extremely busy in these next few months, but should you want to get away one day And play. please give me a call. I'm in the PGA tour directory. Again Congratulations, and Best Regards.

Bob Boyer

HOUSE OF REPRESENTATIVES
WASHINGTON, D. C. 20515

WILLIAM LACY CLAY
FIRST DISTRICT, MISSOURI

January 8, 2002

Mr. Ozzie Smith

Dear Ozzie:

I want to join all St. Louisans in congratulating you on your first-round induction into the Baseball Hall of Fame, an honor of which you are most deserving. Your unique style of play and extraordinary skills redefined the role of shortstop and set a new standard of baseball excellence by which all future shortstops will be judged. Quite simply, you have been and will always be in a league of your own.

I not only congratulate you on your distinguished career and your induction into the Hall of Fame, but I also want to thank you on behalf of all Cardinals fans for the many years of excitement and enjoyment you brought to our team and to this city. All of St. Louis is very proud of you and your accomplishments and wish you all the best for the future.

Sincerely,

Lacy

William Lacy Clay
Member of Congress

NOT PRINTED AT GOVERNMENT E

Alvin and Jackie Dark

Ozzie,

I have been trying to put together my thoughts on paper to express to you how great you made me feel when you invited me to be your guest at your Hall of Fame induction. When I got off the phone with you, my excitement was so great that Jackie thought I had been voted in the Hall. The excitement was for only "You". Praise God that the committee didn't overlook the Greatest SS I have ever seen. Not only on the field, but your character is above reproach.

You can not know what your thinking of having me there with you ment to me. You know the reason I can not be there with you, but I will be there in Spirit.

Love You, Ozzie

Dark

P.S. I have prayed that God will give you the words that He wants you to use to honor our Savior, Jesus Christ. Your friend

A. D.

It all Started...

– Photo's & Clips courtesy of David Simpson

OZZIE SMITH

16 the YUMA ☉ DAILY SUN TUMA ARIZONA Sun., Mar. 4, 1979

'Oz' had superb rookie season at short

When a Cincinnati Reds scout first saw Ozzie Smith play shortstop a few years back he said Smith was "the best shortstop I've ever seen."

But Smith didn't go to the Reds. Instead he went to the San Diego Padres where he figures to stay for many years.

Smith had a superb rookie season in 1978, finishing second to Atlanta Brave third baseman Bob Horner for Rookie of the Year honors. Smith played in 159 of the Padres' 162 games. He led the National League in sacrifice hits with 28 and ended up fourth in stolen bases with 40. However, it was his defense that raised eyebrows.

"Ozzie is the best young infielder I've ever seen," said Padre Manager Roger Craig. "Very soon he's going to be one of the best shortstops in baseball, if not the best."

Smith had 11 games in which he collected three or more hits, including a four-for-four effort June 30 at Houston, and a four-for-four performance July 31 against the Dodgers. Smith had a string of 12 consecutive stolen base attempts from May 20 thru July 5.

Smith showed consistency by batting .259 for the first half of season and .257 the second half. He dropped under .260 on the last day of the season. Smith was drafted by the Padres in June, 1977 and played in Walla Walla, Wash., and batted .303. In the off-season he hit .323 in the Arizona Instructional League where he caught the eye of Padre brass.

Smith played his college ball at Cal Poly-San Luis Obispo.

OZZIE SMITH

Castillo looked good when given opportunity

Tony Castillo is expected to lend the San Diego Padres a hand behind the plate during the 1979 campaign.

The 21-year-old native of San Jose, Calif., showed the Padres he can handle the job during a portion of the 1978 season after being called up in September and playing well defensively during five late-season games.

Prior to joining the Padres he had a disappointing season at Amarillo with a .211 batting average and no homers in 89 games. But in 1977 Castillo had his best offensive season in four professional years, hitting .261 while still at Amarillo.

Castillo joined the Padres as the team's third round selection in the June Free Agent Draft in 1975 out of James Lick High School in San Jose where he hit .297 as a senior, was named his team's MVP and was selected to the All-Mt. Hamilton Athletic League first team. As a high school catcher Castillo allowed only three stolen bases during his prep career.

STATS

Career Batting Statistics

Year	Team	G	AB	R	H	2B	3B	HR	RBI	SO	AVG	SLG	OBP
1978	SDN	159	590	69	152	17	6	1	46	43	.258	.312	.312
1979	SDN	156	587	77	124	18	6	0	27	37	.211	.262	.260
1980	SDN	158	609	67	140	18	5	0	35	49	.230	.276	.315
1981	SDN	110	450	53	100	11	2	0	21	37	.222	.256	.294
1982	SLN	140	488	58	121	24	1	2	43	32	.248	.314	.342
1983	SLN	159	552	69	134	30	6	3	50	36	.243	.335	.323
1984	SLN	124	412	53	106	20	5	1	44	17	.257	.337	.349
1985	SLN	158	537	70	148	22	3	6	54	27	.276	.361	.356
1986	SLN	153	514	67	144	19	4	0	54	27	.280	.333	.378
1987	SLN	158	600	104	182	40	4	0	75	36	.303	.383	.394
1988	SLN	153	575	80	155	27	1	3	51	43	.270	.336	.354
1989	SLN	155	593	82	162	30	8	2	50	37	.273	.361	.337
1990	SLN	143	512	61	130	21	1	1	50	33	.254	.305	.336
1991	SLN	150	550	96	157	30	3	3	50	36	.285	.367	.380
1992	SLN	132	518	73	153	20	2	0	31	34	.295	.342	.367
1993	SLN	141	545	75	157	22	6	1	53	18	.288	.356	.341
1994	SLN	98	381	51	100	18	3	3	30	26	.262	.349	.329
1995	SLN	44	156	16	31	5	1	0	11	12	.199	.244	.286
1996	SLN	82	227	36	64	10	2	2	18	9	.282	.370	.358
19	2	2573	9396	1257	2460	402	69	28	793	589	262	.328	.339

Career Fielding Statistics

Year	Pos	Team	Lg	G	PO	A	E	DP	PCT
1978	SS	SD	NL	159	264	548	25	98	.970
1979	SS	SD	NL	155	256	555	20	86	.976
1980	SS	SD	NL	158	288	621	24	113	.974
1981	SS	SD	NL	10	220	422	16	72	.976
1982	SS	SL	NL	139	279	535	13	101	.984
1983	SS	SL	NL	158	304	519	21	100	.975
1984	SS	SL	NL	124	233	437	12	94	.982
1985	SS	SL	NL	158	264	549	14	111	.983
1986	SS	SL	NL	144	229	453	15	96	.978
1987	SS	SL	NL	158	245	516	10	111	.987
1988	SS	SL	NL	150	234	519	22	79	.972
1989	SS	SL	NL	153	209	483	17	73	.976
1990	SS	SL	NL	140	212	378	12	66	.980
1991	SS	SL	NL	150	244	387	8	79	.987
1992	SS	SL	NL	132	232	420	10	82	.985
1993	SS	SL	NL	134	251	451	19	98	.974
1994	SS	SL	NL	96	135	291	8	67	.982
1995	SS	SL	NL	41	60	129	7	28	.964
1996	SS	SL	NL	52	90	162	8	36	.969
19	1	2	1	2511	4249	8375	281	1590	.978

Career Post Season Batting Statistics

Year	Team	Lg	Playoff	G	AB	R	H	2B	3B	HR	RBI	BB	SO	SB	AVG
1982	STL	N	NLCS	3	9	0	5	0	0	0	3	3	0	1	.556
1985	STL	N	NLCS	6	23	4	10	1	1	1	3	3	1	1	.435
1987	STL	N	NLCS	7	25	2	5	0	1	0	1	3	4	0	.200
1996	STL	N	NLCS	3	9	0	0	0	0	0	0	0	1	0	.000
1996	STL	N	NWDIV	2	3	1	1	0	0	0	0	2	0	0	.333
1982	STL	N	WS	7	24	3	5	0	0	0	1	3	0	1	.208
1985	STL	N	WS	7	23	1	2	0	0	0	0	4	0	1	.087
1987	STL	N	WS	7	28	3	6	0	0	0	2	2	3	2	.214
8	1	1	—	42	144	14	34	1	2	1	10	20	9	6	.236

"I can honestly say that if I asked myself after every game of my career if I had given my best effort and tried my hardest, the answer would be yes. That was the only way I knew how to play."

– Ozzie, May 2002

(AP Photo/Jim McKnight)